About
Skill Builders
Writing Grades 7–8
by Jerry Aten

Welcome to the Skill Builders series. This series is designed to make learning both fun and rewarding.

This workbook holds students' interest with the right mix of humor, imagination, and instruction as they steadily improve their writing skills. The diverse assignments enhance basic writing skills from the idea-gathering process through creating the final written product.

Additionally, a critical-thinking section includes exercises to help develop higher-order thinking skills.

Learning is more effective when approached with enthusiasm. That's why the Skill Builders series combines academically sound exercises with engaging graphics and exciting themes—to make reviewing basic skills at school or at home fun and effective, for both you and your budding scholars.

Credits:
Editor: Sandra Toland
Layout Design: Mark Conrad
Illustrations: Bill Neville
Cover Concept: Nick Greenwood

www.summerbridgeactivities.com

Table of Contents

How to Use This Book

Writing can be broken into several components, and students can become better writers through the development of these components. The activities in this book were developed to follow the traits of good writing and to provide students with the extra practice they may need for each specific writing component.

Ideas: Activities included in this section will help students learn how to create idea lists that lead to topics about which they want to write. Students will also learn how to narrow a broad idea to a workable topic.

Organization: Activities included in this section help students build structure in their writing. Students will learn to define beginnings, middles, and ends in their pieces and to utilize transition and sequencing strategies.

Word Choice: Activities included in this section focus on strengthening students' language skills. Students will discover that vivid words and phrases hold a reader's attention and make finished writing understandable and meaningful.

Fluency: Activities included in this section help students develop a natural rhythm in their writing so that it has a pleasing flow for the reader. Varied sentence length and structure, as well as logical, proper word order, are covered here.

Voice: Activities included in this section focus on teaching students to project their own personalities into their writing. Students learn the importance of writing with a purpose and writing with their own language and thoughts.

Conventions: Activities included in this section allow students to practice the mechanics of writing. Activities enhance students' confidence in accurately punctuating sentences, making appropriate grammar choices, and correctly spelling words.

Critical-Thinking Skills: Activities included in this section stimulate students' higher-level thinking.

All of the activities in this book are versatile. Most are single-page assignments, so they can easily supplement a standard writing curriculum. The writing component covered by each activity is identified at the top of each page for ease of use.

Finally, a list of standard proofreaders' marks has been included at the back of this workbook to assist students in editing their writing.

Brainstorming

One of the first decisions to make in creating a good piece of writing is what to write about. It is sometimes difficult to find a good writing topic, especially on command.

A good strategy to generate ideas is to write down any possibilities that come to mind. For example, imagine that your teacher wants you to write about your favorite time of the year. To get started, you might make each of the four seasons a heading, and then write down events that you enjoy during each season. This technique of generating ideas is called **brainstorming**. It is a great way to begin thinking about a writing topic.

Directions: Imagine that your teacher wants you to write an essay describing your favorite weekend activity. Use the space below to brainstorm ideas for your essay. Use a separate sheet of paper if you need more room.

_____

_____

_____

_____

_____

_____

_____

_____

_____

_____

_____

_____

_____

Idea Clusters

Writers sometimes use the clustering technique, or **concept map**, to help them to visually organize their thoughts. Look at the example below. In the middle of the diagram is an oval labeled *Favorite Time of the Year*, which is the main focus of the assignment.

Note the four ovals representing the seasons that connect to this central idea. The lines that extend from each of these ovals support specific ideas that relate to each of the seasons. A concept map can become as specific or have as many branches as the writer wishes.

Directions: On the lines below, write down details that relate to each of the seasons. Keep adding details until you find an idea for a writing topic.

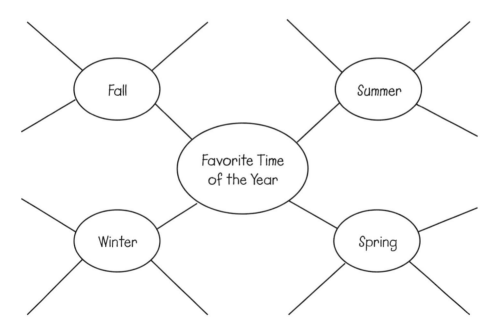

Can you see how visual and organized your thoughts have become?

Now, choose a topic that interests you and create a similar concept map for that topic on a separate sheet of paper. Add as many ovals and lines as you need to accommodate your thoughts.

Fastwriting

When writing about a topic, it is helpful to have a collection of ideas already. One way to start a collection is to keep a notebook for writing ideas. To collect these ideas, set aside a couple of minutes each day to brainstorm. Simply sit down, open a notebook, and write down everything that comes to mind for two minutes. This technique is called **fastwriting**, and writers can use it to generate ideas for future use.

Directions: Try fastwriting in the space below. Use another sheet of paper if you need more room. Write down everything that comes to mind for two minutes. Do not worry about writing in complete sentences or using correct grammar. When the time is up, keep the page and add it to a writing notebook that you can use in the future. Do the same thing again tomorrow. You will be surprised by how many ideas you collect.

_____

_____

_____

_____

_____

_____

_____

_____

_____

_____

_____

_____

Say Cheese!

You have probably heard the phrases, *the story behind the picture*, and *A picture is worth a thousand words*. Both phrases point to the value of **photographs** as sources of writing ideas.

Directions: Look through old photos or scrapbooks. As you search the photos, look for a picture that triggers a fond memory of a special moment. Then, on the lines below, write down every thought you have about why the story behind that picture is special to you. Continue on another sheet of paper if you need more room. Describe the picture in your story.

_____

_____

_____

_____

_____

_____

_____

_____

_____

_____

_____

_____

_____

_____

_____

_____

_____

_____

_____

Thinking Outside the Box

IDEAS

Writers are often expected to think *outside the box*, which means doing some inventive and **creative thinking** to solve a problem or to answer a question in an unusual way. This creative thinking can be used to generate writing ideas.

Directions: For each prompt below, write down three ideas that could become future writing ideas. Try to think *outside the box*. Add this page to your writing notebook.

With a million dollars, I would _____

_____

_____

_____

If I could have one wish, it would be _____

_____

_____

_____

An advantage to living for 200 years would be _____

_____

_____

_____

If I could become an inanimate object, I would be a _____

_____

_____

_____

_____

Changing History

Another strategy writers use to generate ideas is to explore a **significant event in history** that caused dramatic changes. Then, think about how the present might be different had the event never happened. Using this strategy can lead to a great idea for a writing assignment.

Directions: Choose one of the topics listed below. Then, generate as many ideas as you can that highlight how you think history might have been different if the event had never happened. Use the lines below. Continue on another sheet of paper if you need more room.

- the invention of the telephone
- the first Rock-and-Roll song
- the invention of the Internet
- the extinction of dinosaurs
- the discovery of oil for fuel
- the Civil Rights Movement in the United States
- the invention of the automobile

_____

_____

_____

_____

_____

_____

_____

_____

_____

_____

_____

_____

_____

_____

Interpreting a Song

Writing creates new images and new thoughts. It can also create new **interpretations** of another writer's words. A great way to practice this is to listen to the lyrics of an unfamiliar song and think about what message or story the songwriter may have had in mind.

You can find the lyrics to many songs on the Internet. Often the music of a song lends additional insight into the songwriter's message.

Directions: Locate a copy of a song and its lyrics that is particularly interesting to you. Listen to the song and read the lyrics several times. Then, write your interpretation of the songwriter's message below.

Song: _____

Songwriter: _____

Interpretation: _____

_____

_____

_____

_____

_____

_____

_____

_____

_____

_____

_____

_____

From General to Specific

IDEAS

Once a writer has collected a pool of ideas, the next step is to decide which ideas are the most interesting. Who will the audience be? From what point of view should the piece be written? What is the purpose of the piece? Is it a story? A poem? Will it be an essay explaining the steps involved in completing a task? Whatever the assignment is, it will involve **narrowing down** the focus of the topic. That means moving from general or broader ideas to more specific topics.

Directions: Number the topics on each list below from the most general idea to the most specific. Begin with *1* as the most general.

_____ newspaper		_____ Grand Canyon	
_____ popular media		_____ places to visit	
_____ letter to the editor		_____ Arizona	
_____ editorial section		_____ United States national parks	
_____ printed material		_____ desert southwest	

_____ Ford Motors		_____ Italy	
_____ automotive industry		_____ Michelangelo	
_____ steering wheel parts testing		_____ painters	
_____ Flint, Michigan facility		_____ The Renaissance	
_____ quality control department		_____ artists	

Now, go to your lists of brainstormed ideas and find one that is very general. Then, break that idea into topics and number them from the most general to the most specific.

_____

_____

_____

_____

_____

Elaborating on an Idea

IDEAS

Once writers have a good topic, they must **elaborate** on it to give readers a good mental image of their ideas. For example, *The Noisy Dog* gives the reader some information, but it does not provide any description or give a reason as to why the dog is noisy. Answering *who, what, when, where, why,* and *how* gives the reader more information.

The dog (*who*) might be a watch dog (*what*) that barks and howls (*how*) at a shipping dock (*where*) every night at midnight (*when*) because some criminals are smuggling goods on the boats (*why*).

Notice how much more information this elaboration provides. Expanding ideas by answering these questions makes writing more informative and interesting for the reader.

Directions: Expand on the following topics using the strategy demonstrated above.

Coming Home after the Game _____

_____

_____

A Dark Night _____

_____

_____

Snowing _____

_____

_____

A Startling Experience _____

_____

_____

_____

Graphic Organizers

It is sometimes helpful for a writer to prepare a visual or graphic **organizational plan** before writing. Different organizers are more useful for different types of writing.

Directions: Decide which organizer below would be the best to use for each of these topics: *Who Are My Ancestors?*; *Asian and African Elephants*; *The Industrial Revolution*.

Compare and Contrast: Attributes

	A	B	C	D	E	F	G

This organizer is appropriate for _____ .

Time Line:

This organizer is appropriate for _____ .

Tree Diagram:

This organizer is appropriate for _____ .

Graphic Organizers (continued)

ORGANIZATION

Directions: Below are three more **graphic organizers**. Look carefully at the design of each. Then, write down an example of a topic that fits each graphic plan.

Venn Diagram:

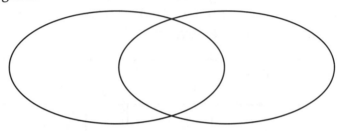

This organizer would work for writing about _____

_____.

Chain of Events:

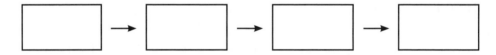

This organizer would work for writing about _____

_____.

Cycle:

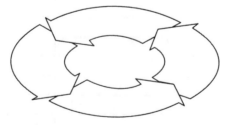

This organizer would work for writing about _____

_____.

Classifying Data

A writer must have an organizational plan to create a good story or informative paper. That plan often involves separating information into categories. One way to do this is to organize data with an **outline**. To create an outline, find the main idea or broad topic first. Next, decide what the subheadings will be. Finally, add the related points and supporting details under each subheading.

Directions: Organize the words in the word bank using the outline below. Then, on a separate sheet of paper, create your own outline with information you gather on the topic of your choice.

Word Bank

cows	mammals	frogs	arachnids	snakes
animals	cardinals	lions	invertebrates	amphibians
crocodiles	spiders	reptiles	mollusks	oysters
scorpions	vertebrates	snails	birds	robins
		salamanders		

I. _____   4. _____

   A. _____   a. _____

      1. _____   b. _____

        a. _____   B. _____

        b. _____   1. _____

      2. _____   a. _____

        a. _____   b. _____

        b. _____   2. _____

      3. _____   a. _____

        a. _____   b. _____

        b. _____

Creating Great Titles

ORGANIZATION

By creating clever **titles**, writers can trigger curiosity in readers and make them want to read more. For example, consider the title *Foiled by a Coil!* Would that title stimulate interest and make a reader want to know how the title fits the reading?

Foiled by a Coil! is about the assassination of United States President James Garfield. When he was shot in 1881, doctors tried to remove the bullet from his body, but they could not locate it. Alexander Graham Bell developed a metal detector that was used to try to find the bullet. However, regardless of where the doctors passed the wand over Garfield's body, the detecting device went off. What the doctors failed to realize was that President Garfield was lying on a new metal coil-spring mattress, so Garfield eventually died of infection.

The title, *Foiled by a Coil!*, is effective because it creates interest and summarizes the story without revealing too much information.

Directions: Read each scenario below. On the lines, write a clever title for each story that does not reveal too much.

A story about a team of mountain climbers scaling a famous mountain:

_____

A different title for the story of *Little Red Riding Hood*:

_____

A story about a seventh-grade student's first day of school in a new city:

_____

A story about a puppy and a lion cub that become best friends:

_____

A story about a scary storm:

_____

Writing a Great Paragraph

A **paragraph** has several related sentences that focus on a single topic or idea. For a paragraph to be effective, it should contain the following elements:

- **Topic sentence**: A good topic sentence states the main idea of the paragraph. Most often, the topic sentence is the first sentence in the paragraph.
- **Supporting sentences**: Details, examples, or indisputable facts should be included to support the topic sentence.
- **Unity and coherence**: Each sentence in the paragraph should focus only on the topic presented in that paragraph's topic sentence. All paragraphs should be written in language that the target audience can easily understand.
- **A transitioning conclusion**: A good concluding sentence summarizes the paragraph and leads the reader into the main idea of the next one.

Directions: Choose one of the following topics. Write a paragraph that includes all of the elements described above. Continue on another sheet of paper if you need more room.

- Regardless of where I travel, there is no place like home.
- The world would be a better place if . . .
- The most valuable lesson I have learned so far is . . .

_____

_____

_____

_____

_____

_____

_____

The Hook

The purpose of a **hook** in writing is to grab the reader's interest right from the beginning. Read the following paragraph.

I had seen hundreds of photographs of them, so I had a general idea of what to expect. But, as I rounded the bend on Route 89 and caught my first glimpse, I realized that if a photo is worth a thousand words, this was worth an entire library. As they came into view, everything changed instantly. My entire view was filled with a beauty that I had never seen before.

Does the paragraph above grab your attention and make you want to read more of the essay?

Directions: For each topic below, write a one- or two-sentence hook that will make your reader want to continue reading your essay.

The most exciting thing I ever experienced: _____

_____

_____

_____

My most memorable vacation: _____

_____

_____

_____

The first time I saw a: _____

_____

_____

The Launch

There are several techniques that a writer can use effectively to pull the reader into an essay. Some techniques that writers use to **launch** their writing include:

- a quotation that stimulates thought
- a question that triggers the curiosity of the reader
- an anecdote or a personal story that sets the mood of what is coming later in the essay
- a dramatic beginning that grabs the reader's full attention

Directions: Choose three of the four strategies listed above. Using these strategies, write three different beginnings on the lines below for a story about an incident you will never forget. Continue on another sheet of paper if you need more room.

1. _____

_____

_____

_____

2. _____

_____

_____

_____

3. _____

_____

_____

_____

The Order of Details

Writers must decide in which **order** to present events to the reader. Order is especially important if the purpose of the essay is to show the reader how to perform a task. For example, if the writer wants to explain to the reader how to build a birdhouse from scraps of wood, the writer should present the steps in the proper order, from choosing pieces of wood to hanging the birdhouse.

However, there are occasions when presenting the events out of order can add mystery to writing. For example, if you were writing an essay entitled *The First Zoos*, you might begin with a scene from a modern zoo, then write about how the first zoos were different. Doing this will create interest for the reader.

Directions: On the lines below, write a paragraph about an event that you have recently experienced. Purposely write about the event out of order to create a more interesting paragraph. Continue on another sheet of paper if you need more room.

_____

_____

_____

_____

_____

_____

_____

_____

_____

_____

_____

The Middle

While both the beginning and the end of an essay are important, it is the **middle** of the essay that contains the real substance. The middle must flow smoothly from one idea to another in proper sequence and style. Creating this flow will keep the reader's attention and ensure that he understands the sequence of events.

Directions: The steps listed below tell how to make decorated sugar cookies, but they are in no particular order. Number the steps in order, starting with *1* as the first step.

_____ Place dough shapes 1" apart on a cookie sheet.

_____ Use cookie cutters to cut the dough into shapes.

_____ Beat eggs and vanilla into the butter and sugar mixture.

_____ Cover the dough mixture with a cloth.

_____ Place dough mixture in the refrigerator and chill for one hour.

_____ Bake cookies for 6–8 minutes.

_____ Decorate cooled cookies with frosting and sprinkles.

_____ Roll the dough out to ¼" to ½" thickness.

_____ In a large bowl, cream together butter and sugar until smooth.

_____ Preheat the oven to 400°F (200°C).

_____ Stir flour, baking powder, and salt into the egg and butter mixture.

_____ Place the chilled dough on a floured surface.

_____ Allow cookies to cool completely.

In Conclusion

The **conclusion** is the part of an essay that summarizes the main points the writer has made. The conclusion does not have to be dramatic, but it should be intriguing enough to keep the reader's attention until the very end. Below are some ways to bring an essay to a good conclusion.

- Use a relevant quotation.
- Close with a question for the reader to think about.
- Provide a hint or a clue as to what might happen in the future.
- Leave an issue open-ended to encourage the reader to draw her own conclusions.
- End with a challenge for action or an inspirational thought.

Directions: Locate an essay that you have written recently. First, reread your essay. Then, use one of the strategies listed above to rewrite your conclusion on a separate sheet of paper. Identify the technique you chose to use, and tell why you made this choice.

Topic of the essay I wrote: _____

Conclusion to that essay: _____

_____

_____

_____

_____

Technique I am using for my new conclusion: _____

_____

Why I chose this strategy and how it made my conclusion better:

_____

_____

My Favorite Words

We all have **favorite words** that we like because of the way they sound or what they describe. Some words are just fun to say. Favorite words can be any part of speech.

Directions: On the lines below, brainstorm for 10 minutes and write down any words that you like. There is no limit to the number of words that you can include. You should be able to write 30–40 words in 10 minutes.

Using My Favorite Words

Directions: Refer back to the list of favorite words you brainstormed in *My Favorite Words* (page 23). From that list, circle 8–10 words that you especially like. Then, on the lines below, write a short story using those words. Use another sheet of paper if you need more room. When you are finished, share your story with a parent or a friend. Tell your reader about the assignment. Is your reader able to identify your favorite words?

_____

_____

_____

_____

_____

_____

_____

_____

_____

_____

_____

_____

_____

_____

_____

_____

_____

Using Vivid Verbs

The right **verb** can be the most descriptive part of speech in a sentence. In fact, sometimes a verb can be so powerful that no other words are needed. For example:

Marnie said to her little brother, "*Leave* my room."
Marnie told her little brother, "*Scram*!"

Which verb in the above sentences gives a more powerful image of Marnie's emotions?

Directions: Replace each italicized verb in the sentences below with a more vivid verb. Write the new verb on the line.

1. _____ Right after class, Jason *left* the school grounds on an important mission.

2. _____ It *frustrates* me to have made so many grammatical mistakes in my essay.

3. _____ We can still get to Grandma's house before dark if you *go* faster.

4. _____ No one from our school *has done* better than third place in that event before.

5. _____ Weak verbs sometimes *need* adverbs to make them more descriptive.

6. _____ The fresh smell of flowers *was* in the room everywhere we went.

7. _____ Barry hit a home run that *traveled* over 450 feet.

8. _____ Cindy leaped high and *put* the ball through the basket.

Words for the Senses

Adjectives are often used to describe the reactions of our senses to outside influences. Writing that the host served a *fiery salsa* gives the reader a better sense of the taste than simply writing *salsa*. Likewise, *the thunderous roar of the raging river* is more descriptive of what someone standing near a large river would hear. A vivid adjective can be the most effective word choice when describing something that the senses reveal.

Directions: Write three adjectives that each sense below might detect. Then, choose one adjective from each sense and write an original sentence that makes good use of the word.

Taste: _____

_____

_____

Smell: _____

_____

_____

Sound: _____

_____

_____

Sight: _____

_____

_____

Touch: _____

_____

_____

Words That Say It All

When writers choose just the right nouns, adjectives, adverbs, and verbs, their essays can become very **powerful**. For example, a writer creating a brochure that advertises home-building sites in the desert might use phrases and statements like:

- a green oasis in the desert
- celebrating its beautiful desert environment
- towering saguaros and other statuesque plants native to the desert
- structures painted in a palette of earth tones with vivid accents of purple, teal, and lavender

Using descriptive language like this can hold a potential home buyer's attention and help sell the product.

Directions: Professional advertisement writers make a living by crafting clever copy to sell their clients' products. Locate an example from either printed media or television that you consider to be clever because of the language the writer used. Describe your example below. Continue on another sheet of paper if you need more room.

_____

_____

_____

_____

_____

_____

_____

_____

_____

_____

Writing to the Senses

WORD CHOICE

Writers use **descriptive language** to capture the characteristics of what they are writing about. Writing will be more realistic if it stimulates the senses of the reader. Since this appeal must come from mental images, the words a writer chooses must be just right. The best way to improve descriptive skill is to practice writing for the senses.

Directions: Choose one setting from the list below and write a paragraph that describes it. Be sure your description uses at least three or more of the five senses. Continue on another sheet of paper if you need more room. When you are finished, have a parent or friend read your paragraph and tell you what senses you included.

- a cemetery
- a bakery
- a seaside cottage
- a crowded shopping mall
- an automobile repair shop
- a wild animal preserve
- a busy restaurant
- a large airport

As Red as a Rose

WORD CHOICE

A **simile** is a comparison of two different things. Usually, the word *like* or *as* is used to show the comparison. Writers use similies as a clever way to describe something and to make their writing more interesting and entertaining. Using similes adds color to a sentence and gives the reader a visual image of the comparison.

For example, the sentence *Alyssa's lips are as red as a rose* tells the reader just how red Alyssa's lips are. Comparing Alyssa's lips to a rose helps to create that image in the reader's mind.

Directions: Circle the words or phrases that are being compared in the sentences below. Then, underline the words that are used to make the comparison.

1. Every time I go into his office, I am like a bug under a magnifying glass.

2. I could hear the coyote's howl as clear as a bell.

3. Once Ian turned in his test paper, he felt as free as a bird.

4. After Nathan paid admission to the park, his wallet was as flat as a pancake.

5. Kelly always seems as happy as a lark.

6. That assignment was like a walk in the park.

7. The sight of land was as welcome as an oasis in the desert.

8. When Carlotta had the flu, she was as sick as a dog.

9. Todd's golf shot was as straight as an arrow.

10. Michelle and Carley are like two peas in a pod.

The Meaning of Metaphors

WORD CHOICE

A **metaphor** is another type of a comparison, but it is less obvious than a simile. Metaphors do not use the words *like* or *as*. Thus, the comparison is not as direct. Read the example below.

Kevin followed in his father's footsteps.

Kevin did not actually follow his father around and step where his father had just stepped. The metaphor means that Kevin followed a path in life similar to that of his father.

Directions: Read the sentences below. On the lines, briefly explain the meaning of each metaphor.

1. Darkness was a cover for their escape. _____

_____

2. Jane's comment really ruffled Kyle's feathers. _____

_____

3. Dad was a bear when he skipped breakfast. _____

_____

4. In the summer, our minds sometimes go flabby. _____

_____

5. Samuel used his eagle eye to spot Cara's missing earring.

_____

6. She paved the way for women in sports. _____

_____

7. Kyle knows so much trivia, he is a walking encyclopedia.

_____

The Meaning of Metaphors (continued)

WORD CHOICE

8. Our new goalie was still green. _____

   _____

9. My mom is a rock in times of crisis. _____

   _____

10. Her memory of the incident was cloudy. _____

    _____

11. The party died after the guest of honor left. _____

    _____

12. Aunt Polly was able to unravel the problem. _____

    _____

13. His thinking is all over the place. _____

    _____

14. Kiki was a shining example of patience. _____

    _____

15. It looks to me like Jamie has slipped a cog. _____

    _____

16. The crowd gave us a warm welcome. _____

    _____

17. Jason was a proud peacock when the curtain went up at his

    daughter's concert. _____

    _____

Changing the Start

Making sentences **flow** from one to the next makes a story or an essay interesting to the reader. One way to accomplish this is to start different sentences with different parts of speech. Different words and phrases at the beginning of each sentence can make the essay flow smoothly and naturally.

Directions: Write a five-sentence paragraph. Each sentence should begin with a different part of speech. Use the list below in any order you choose. Continue on another sheet of paper if you need more room.

- an adjective (Do not start with an article: *a*, *an*, or *the*.)
- a verb that ends in –ing
- a noun
- a preposition
- an adverb

_____

_____

_____

_____

_____

_____

_____

_____

_____

_____

_____

Changing the Finish

Writers can add interest to their pieces by changing the way they end sentences. Ending sentences with different parts of speech can add **dynamics** to an essay or a story. Read the examples below.

He who hesitates is *lost*. (adjective)
She who hesitates *loses*. (verb)
The one who hesitates will be the *loser*. (noun)
The one who hesitates will come in *last*. (adverb)
To hesitate will cost *him*. (pronoun)

Ending each sentence with a different part of speech adds variety to writing. The sentence will say the same thing, but it will say it in a different way.

Directions: Choose one of the following proverbs. On another sheet of paper, rewrite the proverb five times to end with the parts of speech listed below. Then, decide which sentence you think is the most powerful and circle it.

- Goodness is better than beauty.
- Look before you leap.
- Beggars cannot be choosers.
- The grass is always greener on the other side of the fence.

1. verb
2. adverb
3. pronoun
4. noun
5. adjective

Building Bridges with Words

Writers must be sure that their readers can follow their line of thinking. They do this by using words that connect one thought or idea to the next. Such words are called **transitions**. As transitions link one thought or idea to the next, they act like bridges that connect the land on both sides of a river. Transitions also connect sentences and paragraphs throughout an essay.

When writing an argumentative essay, the writer must use words that provide a transition back and forth between ideas and supporting points. Words and phrases like *however, by comparison, conversely*, and *on the other hand* show comparison or contrast.

Directions: On the lines below, write more words or phrases that you can use to compare or contrast one idea or thought to another.

_____

_____

Another strategy writers use to connect ideas in an essay is to signal that there is more information for a reader. Phrases like *in addition to* and *equally important* are examples of transitions that promise to give a reader additional information about a topic.

On the lines below, write more words or phrases that a writer uses to give the reader additional information.

_____

_____

When a writer wants to show time sequence or the steps involved in performing a task, he uses words like *first, second, third, next*, and *finally*.

On the lines below, write more words or phrases that show sequence.

_____

_____

Building Bridges with Words (continued)

FLUENCY

Writers use words and phrases like *for example* and *in this situation* to signal an example for the reader.

On the lines below, write other words or phrases that signal that the writer is giving an example.

_____

_____

Transitions such as *in conclusion* and *to summarize* signal to the reader that the writer will be bringing an essay to a close. The concluding transition will also let the reader know if there is one more point (*finally*) or if there is a summary to follow (*in summary*).

On the lines below, write more words or phrases that show that the essay is coming to a close.

_____

_____

Words like *obviously*, *evidently*, *definitely*, and *unquestionably* emphasize a point and reflect the writer's opinion.

On the lines below, write more words or phrases that you can use to emphasize your opinion or to make a point.

_____

_____

Phrases like *next to*, *across the street from*, and directional words like *southeast* identify location.

On the lines below, write more words or phrases that show location.

_____

_____

On the Other Hand

Directions: Refer to the explanations and examples of transition words and phrases that you listed in *Building Bridges with Words* (pages 34–35). Match the transition words and phrases below to the various situations in which they should be used. Write the letter of the appropriate situation on the blank line before each transition.

A. comparing or contrasting
B. providing more information
C. time sequencing
D. providing emphasis
E. giving an example
F. signaling a conclusion

1. _____ as I have shown

2. _____ in contrast

3. _____ furthermore

4. _____ following this

5. _____ to summarize

6. _____ in this case

7. _____ without a doubt

8. _____ and then

9. _____ on the contrary

10. _____ to illustrate

11. _____ in addition

12. _____ simultaneously

13. _____ moreover

14. _____ obviously

15. _____ inarguably

16. _____ in the same manner

17. _____ however

18. _____ in this situation

19. _____ conversely

20. _____ unquestionably

21. _____ previously

22. _____ as the evidence shows

23. _____ by which I mean

24. _____ finally

Varying Sentence Length

One way to vary sentences is to **rearrange** the words. Many times, the parts of a sentence can be moved to other places in the sentence and still make sense. For example:

Susan went to the park yesterday with her little sister.
Yesterday, Susan went to the park with her little sister.
With her little sister, Susan went to the park yesterday.

Directions: On the lines provided, rewrite the sentence below in two different ways. Use words and phrases that will make the sentence more interesting. Vary the length and add details, but do not lose the meaning of the original sentence.

The new kid in our class is a really good athlete.

1. _____

   _____

2. _____

   _____

A writer can also add variety to a piece by **combining** several shorter sentences into one long sentence.

On the lines provided, combine the two sentences below in two different ways. Add or delete words and phrases to make the sentences more interesting, but do not change the meaning of the original sentences.

Mark studied harder than ever before. It really paid off.

1. _____

   _____

2. _____

   _____

Building a Better Sentence

Writers can make their sentences better and more interesting by adding details that answer such questions as *When? Where? What kind? Which one? How often? To what degree? How did it happen?* Read the two sentences below.

- Elaine went for a walk.
- Elaine took her dog, Buster, for a long walk last Saturday all of the way around Lake Rose, and they did not get back home until nearly dark.

The added details in the second sentence answer the questions *Where did she go? What did she do? When did she do it? How far did she go? With whom did she go? How long did she walk?* The reader has a much more **vivid** description of Elaine's walk in the second sentence than in the first.

Directions: On the lines provided, rewrite each sentence below to make it better by adding pieces of information and description that address the questions in parentheses.

1. We went to the mall. (Why? When? How?) _____

   _____

   _____

2. Laurie got her test back. (When? What grade? What kind of test?)

   _____

   _____

   _____

3. Andre asked his mom for a ride. (Why? When? Where?) _____

   _____

   _____

Restructuring Sentences

Good writing involves careful **editing**. An important step in editing a piece of writing is to focus on the composition and structure of sentences. Reread each sentence and ask, *How can I make this sentence better?* During the editing process, the final goal of the writer is to make the essay into a polished, finished piece.

Directions: Read the sentences below. While each sentence is grammatically correct, you can make it better by adding or changing words and phrases. You can also rewrite the entire sentence. Write your new, better sentence on the lines provided.

1. You do not have to remember what you said if you tell the truth.

   _____

   _____

   _____

2. Rise to the occasion when you are given a challenge.

   _____

   _____

3. The moments in life that take our breath away are more important than the number of breaths we take.

   _____

   _____

   _____

4. You will know what you are worth if you pay as you owe.

   _____

   _____

   _____

Evaluating Fluency

Directions: Read the following passage. Answer the questions below the passage about the flow and **quality** of the writing.

My New Friend

I want to tell you a story about my new friend Callie. She come to our class from Massachusetts. I moved here to one time from somewheres else. Anyway, Callie seemed shy when she came to room. I member that feeling myself when I got here. Anyway, Mrs. Schultz said who she was and told Callie to set down wherever she saw an empty seat. I smiled at her so she set down acrost the isle from me. We talked a while and she asked my name. When the bell rung, I asked her to come to lunch with me. We set down by nobody and talked alot. We become pretty good friends by afternoon. She give me her fone number so we could talk at night. We're friends now. I like her lot.

1. What is your opinion about the sentence structure?

   _____

   _____

2. If you were asked to edit this paragraph, what steps would you take to improve the flow from one sentence to the next?

   _____

   _____

3. If you were to correct the worst errors first, where would you start?

   _____

   _____

4. If you were to rank the writing quality from 1 (very poor) to 10 (excellent), what number value would you assign? Why?

   _____

Repetition

Writers sometimes repeat words and phrases to emphasize their points and to make a more powerful impact on the reader. Note the **repetition** in the closing statements of Dr. Martin Luther King Jr.'s *I Have a Dream* speech.

"And let freedom ring from the prodigious hilltops of New Hampshire. Let freedom ring from the mighty mountains of New York. Let freedom ring from the heightening Alleghenies of Pennsylvania. Let freedom ring from the snow-capped Rockies of Colorado. Let freedom ring from the curvaceous slopes of California."

Furthermore, note the repetition in President Abraham Lincoln's *Gettysburg Address*.

"[W]e can not dedicate—we can not consecrate—we can not hallow—this ground . . . and that government of the people, by the people, for the people, shall not perish from the earth."

How much less dramatic would the speeches above have been without the use of repetition? While repetition can be a powerful tool in the hands of a writer, there are other times when repetition is not effective and may even detract from the message.

Directions: Read each situation below. Decide whether you think repetition would be an effective technique to get the message across to an audience. Write *yes* or *no* on the line before each situation.

1. _____ You are given a writing assignment on one of your favorite things to do: "I love going to the beach. I love the sand between my toes. I love . . . "

2. _____ An ad agency is asked to create copy for a one-minute television commercial for a local cell-phone dealer: "More area coverage. More features. More . . . "

Playing with Language

Songwriters often use the techniques of alliteration and assonance to add interest to their writing. It can make their work flow naturally and sound almost conversational.

Alliteration is the repetition of the same consonant sound at the beginning of two or more words in the same sentence. Some of the more exaggerated uses of alliteration are called *tongue twisters*. For example:

Julie Jensen juggled the juicy, jiggly jellyfish.

The *j* sound at the beginning of several words in a row helps add punch to the above sentence.

Directions: Read the sentences below. Place a check mark next to the sentences that you consider alliterative.

_____ I go there. I went there.
_____ The rafters raced down Red Rock River.
_____ The moon smiles back at you.
_____ I listen to the wind.
_____ See the sun shine.
_____ Bye, bye, baby, goodbye.

On the lines below, write a list of words that begin with the letter *m*.

_____

_____

Now, write an alliterative sentence using some of the *m* words you listed above.

_____

_____

_____

Playing with Language (continued)

FLUENCY

Assonance is the repetition of vowel sounds in words that may begin with different consonants. Such words are a bit more difficult to locate, but they provide writers with yet another play on language that makes the written word more interesting and lasting for the reader. For example:

That child of mine cried, lying on his side in the night.

What vowel sound is repeated in this sentence? It is the long-*i* sound.

Directions: Read the phrases below. If the phrase is an example of assonance, write the vowel sound on the line before the phrase. If the phrase is not an example of assonance, write *no* on the line.

_____ find a bin to put it in

_____ red, red robin, comes bob, bob, bobbin'

_____ pick up a penny and make it your own

_____ squealing tires on the wet pavement

_____ Ease between the trees; he can squeeze to be unseen.

Now, write two phrases of your own that use assonance.

_____

_____

Explain a situation in your own writing where either assonance or alliteration (or both) could be used effectively.

_____

_____

_____

_____

Making Voices Heard

Identifying the audience is one of a writer's first concerns when planning an essay. Once that decision has been made, the writer must then craft words and sentences that make a piece of writing appeal to the reader. For example, an editorial in a local newspaper urging people to re-elect the county sheriff would include character traits that are supportive, loyal, patriotic, honest, and professional. Well-chosen words and phrases that include a combination of these **character traits** will go a long way in convincing the reader to vote for the writer's choice.

Directions: Write an essay on a topic of your choice. First, identify the audience to whom you are directing your essay. Then, choose one or more of the character traits from the list below. Write your essay on a separate sheet of paper, using language that reflects the traits you chose. Finally, underline the specific words and phrases you used to make the character traits heard.

Character Traits

professional	clever	warm	patient
intelligent	grateful	hard working	courageous
passionate	humble	hard nosed	subtle
dedicated	caring	kind	tough
honest	unselfish	proud	candid

My topic: _____

_____

My audience: _____

Character Traits I will use: _____

_____

_____

_____

What Is the Purpose?

Another concern that writers must address before they start writing is to define the **purpose** of an essay.

- Is he trying to persuade someone?
- Is she comparing one thing with another?
- Is he trying to predict what will happen as a result of some future event?
- Is she defending her position on a controversial issue?
- Is he trying to analyze, explain, or evaluate someone or something?

It is important to be clear about the purpose of the essay before starting to write, because that purpose will determine the mood and structure of the writing. Sentence structure, word choice, and the mood of the piece are all directly related to the writer's purpose.

Directions: Read each description of various pieces of writing below. Decide what you think the writer's purpose is from the list above. Write your choice on the lines provided.

1. A teacher responds to the parent of a student who asked for reasons why his child received a failing grade in her class.

   _____

2. A student wants to tell others how to make a homemade pizza.

   _____

3. A mother writes an e-mail to her child away at college to ask about recent mysterious and hefty credit-card charges.

   _____

4. A science student prepares to write down what she thinks will happen when she performs an experiment in science class.

   _____

Writing with a Purpose

VOICE

Directions: Choose one of the purposes for writing listed on *What is the Purpose?* (page 45). On the lines provided, write a short essay based on the purpose you chose. You may write about any topic, as long as you clearly define your purpose in the first paragraph. Make statements throughout your essay that accomplish that purpose. Continue on another sheet of paper if you need more room. When you are finished writing your essay, share your writing with a friend or a parent. Ask them to state what they believe to be your purpose for writing the essay.

_____

_____

_____

_____

_____

_____

_____

_____

_____

_____

_____

_____

_____

_____

_____

_____

_____

This Really Is Me!

VOICE

Voice is the personality of a writer. Every person is different, so the voice of every writer is different. It is important for a reader to feel a writer's personality in the writing. If this happens, the reader will be more inclined to connect with what a writer has to say. Allowing feelings and emotions to rise to the surface of an essay will capture a reader's attention. Whether a reader agrees with a writer or not, the writing will still be interesting to a reader. The language a writer uses will bring the voice to life for the reader.

Directions: Finish each of the statements below with words, phrases, and comments that tell the reader that you are the writer. Be honest and make your own voice be heard.

I am saddened when I hear _____

_____

_____

_____

If I were a place on Earth, I would be _____

_____

because _____

_____

_____

My biggest concern is _____

_____

_____

I want people to remember me for _____

_____

_____

The Blank Card

VOICE

A handwritten, personal note from the sender of a card is more meaningful than a message prepared by a greeting card company. This is because the note has the **voice** of the sender, not a generic tone. Blank cards are especially nice to send for this reason, because writers can put their own personalities into their messages and tailor them to a specific situation or occasion.

Directions: Design your own card on the lines below. First, decide who you will be sending the card to and for what occasion.Then, decide on a picture for the front of the card. Blank cards often have beautiful or funny photos or other attractive artwork on the fronts. Be as specific as possible when describing your picture. Finally, write your personal message to the recipient of your card.

Occasion: _____

Recipient: _____

Picture on the front: _____

_____

_____

_____

Message: _____

_____

_____

_____

_____

_____

_____

_____

Active Voice vs. Passive Voice

VOICE

An important aspect of writing is deciding whether to use the **active** voice or the **passive** voice. Using the verb in the active voice adds power to a sentence and makes writing more direct. However, there are situations where the passive voice is required, such as when the sentence would be too awkward in the active voice.

Changing the voice of the verb can change the tone of the sentence. Understanding how to recognize and use each voice is another step toward good writing. Read the examples below.

- **Active voice**: Americans *charged* over $3 billion during the holiday season.
- **Passive voice**: Over $3 billion *was charged* by Americans during the holiday season.

In the active voice, *charged* is the verb and *Americans* are committing the action. In the passive voice, *were charged* is the verb and the subject, *$3 billion*, receives the action.

Directions: On a separate sheet of paper, rewrite each of the sentences below from passive voice to active voice. Additional information may need to be added to the sentence to make the change.

1. The Madison County Courthouse was built in 1837 when the county seat was moved to Madison.

2. Martin Hennessey was sent to the nurse's office by Ms. Kirsch because he fainted in class.

3. Kaori's mom was recently named CEO at the company where she works.

4. My sister Julia was crowned Hamilton High School Homecoming Queen at the dance last night.

5. Brent and Steven were declared co-champions after 10 straight free throws were made by them in the playoff game.

From a Different Perspective

Voice must be considered when writing dialogue. If a writer creates a character different from herself, then that character must have a distinct voice and a realistic personality. Everything depends on the **perspective**. Consider the following statements made by six-year-olds when they were asked, *What is a grandparent?*

- "They are so old they shouldn't play hard or run."
- "When they take us for walks, they slow down past things like pretty leaves and caterpillars."
- "They don't say, 'Hurry up!'"
- "When they read to us, they don't skip. They don't mind if we ask for the same story over again."
- "They show us and talk to us about the color of the flowers and also why we shouldn't step on sidewalk cracks."
- "Grandparents don't have to do anything except be there when we come to see them."
- "They know we should have snack time before bedtime and they kiss us even when we've acted badly."
- "Everybody should try to have a grandmother, especially if you don't have TV."

Directions: Try your own hand at writing from the perspective of a six-year-old. Choose one of the topics below. On a separate sheet of paper, write dialogue that might be said by a six-year-old character on one of the topics listed below.

- why adults are always in a hurry
- what it means to be a friend
- what a good job really is
- why it will be fun to be an adult
- why I want to stay a kid
- what it means to be a parent
- how to take care of a pet

Effective Dialogue

Dialogue is used so that characters can communicate with each other. Dialogue can reveal a character's personality much better than merely telling the reader about a character. It is important to realize that dialogue is not just characters in a story talking. Everyday exchanges, such as "Hi Anne, how are you?" and "I am fine" tell a reader nothing about the characters.

Directions: Choose one of the story titles below. On the lines provided, write a short play using the title you chose. Focus on two characters and craft their words to reveal their thoughts, motives, and feelings. Continue on a separate sheet of paper if you need more room.

- Lending a Hand
- A Surprise Guest
- A Lost Treasure
- Hero for a Day

_____

_____

_____

_____

_____

_____

_____

_____

_____

_____

_____

_____

_____

Narrative Voice

VOICE

Voice is important to consider when writing a narrative. The writer must decide who is telling the story. If the narrator is telling the story as though it is happening to him, the story is written in **first person**. Pronouns like *I*, *my*, *me*, and *we* will appear often.

Sometimes, the writer chooses to talk about the subject rather than to relate it in first person. When this happens, a narrator tells the story in **third person**. In this case, the writer will use pronouns like *he*, *she*, *it*, and *they*.

At other times, it might look like the writer uses both the first person and the third person. When readers see this, it means that the story is actually in first person. For example:

> I went to her house to pick her up. But, Maggie had already left for school.

The second sentence looks like it is in third person. But, the story is written in first person because the first sentence includes the pronoun *I*. If even one sentence is in first person, then the entire story is written in first person.

Directions: Read each sentence below. Write *1* on the line if the sentence is written in first person. Write *3* on the line if the sentence is written in third person.

1. _____ Many of my friends like horror movies, but I do not!

2. _____ Frank Carmen brought oranges from Florida for all of his neighbors.

3. _____ My dog was never formally trained, but he does everything I tell him to do.

4. _____ I feel a wonderful sense of accomplishment when I get a good grade on a test.

5. _____ Cam gave his grandmother a hug before he boarded the train.

First-Person Point of View

Directions: Choose one of the characters below. On the lines provided, write a short paragraph about an event or an incident using the character you chose as the first-person narrator. Your paragraph can be part of a bigger story, or it can be a one-paragraph piece. Continue on another sheet of paper if you need more room.

- an electrician installing a light fixture
- a weary teacher at 4:00 P.M. on Friday
- the best basketball player at a pep rally
- the city's spelling champion
- a local TV weather person
- a student talking to his parents about a bad grade
- a child having an imaginary tea party

_____

_____

_____

_____

_____

_____

_____

_____

_____

_____

_____

_____

_____

_____

_____

Personal Narrative Writing

When writing **personal narratives**, writers draw on their own experiences to make the stories real for their readers. Readers should be able to relate to the events in a narrative. A personal narrative is told in first-person point of view and involves the reader in the writer's emotions during that experience.

Directions: Choose one of the topics below. On the lines provided, write a personal narrative about the topic you chose. Continue on another sheet of paper if you need more room.

- the strangest thing I ever saw
- a trip to my favorite restaurant
- how I solved a problem
- how I spent a memorable day
- a time when I was afraid
- when I learned how to . . .

_____

_____

_____

_____

_____

_____

_____

_____

_____

_____

_____

_____

_____

_____

Noticing the Little Things

VOICE

Paying attention to the **details** helps writers put their personalities into their writing and makes it more enjoyable to read. Providing details will give a reader a much better mental image of what is being described or explained. Even the details that may not seem important will sound impressive if the writer brings each thought into full focus. Read the example below.

As I stepped through the French doors, I knew immediately that I was in a very special place. Flowers and plants were everywhere. Beautiful dark green vines clung to the cream-colored stucco wall behind the patio. The flagstone paving blended perfectly with the surrounding garden walls. In the far corner was a tall, stately, old oak tree that I had climbed when I was a little boy. Grandpa had obviously made it the showpiece of the entire landscape.

The writer has chosen his words carefully to put the reader in this place and to see and feel what he saw and felt at that moment.

Directions: Choose a moment from your past and describe it on the lines below. Use words and phrases that show you are paying close attention to the details. Let your voice shine through. Continue on another sheet of paper if you need more room.

_____

_____

_____

_____

_____

_____

_____

_____

Descriptive Writing

Writing is the opposite of *Show and Tell*. In *Show and Tell*, a student has a physical object to **show** and **describe** to classmates. In writing, the object is not present for the reader to see. That is why the writer must show the audience the object or scene using vivid words and description.

For example, the sentence *The tornado was really scary!* is a *telling* statement. Even though the sentence gives the reader information about the tornado, it does not *show* the reader just how scary the tornado really was. The passage below gives more detail and *shows* the writer's experience.

My parents had told me what to do if I ever heard the siren. I was too far away to run for home, which had been their first instruction. I looked over my shoulder into the southwestern sky, and there it was! A huge, dark cloud shaped like a funnel was headed my way! I ran into the closest building I could find. It was the library. The librarian told me to get down underneath one of the big tables. Then, I heard it—a huge roar that sounded like a train was right outside of the library! I closed my eyes and crouched down even further. I tightened my grip on my knees with my head buried between them.

Directions: Choose one of the *telling* statements below. On a separate sheet of paper, write a brief descriptive essay to *show* your reader the statement. Use detailed and vivid description to help the reader create a clear mental image.

- I went to a pretty flower garden.
- My room is comfortable to me.
- Riding on an airplane is exciting.
- The beach is a fun place to visit.
- Going to a baseball game is better than watching it on television.

Persuasive Writing

The purpose of **persuasive** writing is to convince the reader to agree with the writer. While writers may present the opposite side of an issue for the reader's information, they do so in a way that makes their own positions very clear. The best way to develop a convincing argument is by using facts and examples for support.

Directions: Choose one of the questions below. On the lines provided, write a brief persuasive essay arguing for your position on the question. Continue on another sheet of paper if you need more room.

- Are locker searches an invasion of privacy?
- Are middle school students assigned too much homework?
- Should students have a curfew on weekends?
- Is it fair to require students to earn good grades before they are allowed to participate in extracurricular activities?
- Does wearing a uniform restrict a student's freedom of expression or individuality?

_____

_____

_____

_____

_____

_____

_____

_____

_____

_____

_____

Expository Writing

The purpose of **expository** writing is to explain, to compare and contrast, to show cause and effect, to provide the reader with information, or to clarify a subject. A good piece of expository writing has a clear and central focus.

Directions: Choose a topic below. Write a brief expository essay about the topic on the lines provided. Continue on another sheet of paper if you need more room.

- my favorite kind of music
- the best aspects of each season
- what I have learned about myself
- my most prized possession
- the life cycle of a butterfly
- how germs are spread

_____

_____

_____

_____

_____

_____

_____

_____

_____

_____

_____

_____

_____

_____

What Part of Speech?

Directions: Read each sentence below. Circle the underlined word that is the **part of speech** listed before the sentence.

1. **adjective**: Mary Jane <u>fell</u> <u>last</u> night and <u>broke</u> her <u>arm</u>.

2. **adverb**: <u>Thomas</u> <u>actively</u> pursued a career as <u>a</u> <u>lawyer</u>.

3. **verb**: Jason's <u>mom</u> <u>won</u> <u>a</u> marathon <u>last</u> year.

4. **conjunction**: I like the <u>taste</u> <u>of</u> sausage pizza, <u>but</u> I like pepperoni <u>better</u>.

5. **preposition**: The <u>soldier</u> <u>gave</u> three years <u>of</u> <u>his</u> life to proudly serve his country.

6. **adverb**: Maggie <u>carefully</u> buried her <u>bone</u> in <u>our</u> <u>backyard</u>.

7. **interjection**: <u>Wow</u>! <u>Whoever</u> heard of <u>such</u> a <u>crazy</u> thing?

8. **preposition**: If you get <u>here</u> <u>by</u> <u>noon</u>, you can ride with <u>us</u>.

9. **adjective**: My Aunt Patricia <u>was</u> hired <u>by</u> Mr. Boynton to <u>be</u> our <u>school</u> secretary.

10. **pronoun**: Does <u>anyone</u> <u>here</u> need <u>an</u> <u>extra</u> sandwich?

11. **noun**: <u>Homer</u> <u>donated</u> blood to help <u>disaster</u> victims <u>in</u> Asia.

12. **verb**: Kelly <u>ran</u> the race in <u>record</u> <u>time</u> for her <u>age</u> group.

13. **preposition**: Mr. Hawthorne has <u>issued</u> <u>a</u> <u>challenge</u> <u>to</u> all of us.

14. **conjunction**: <u>Carley</u> asked her mom <u>for</u> a new bike <u>and</u> a helmet for <u>her</u> birthday.

The Proper Use of Commas

Directions: Read each rule below describing the proper use of **commas**. On the lines provided, write a sentence that shows the correct use of each comma rule.

1. **Compound sentences**: A comma is placed before the coordinating conjunction in a compound sentence.

   _____

   _____

2. **Items in a series:** Commas are used to separate words, phrases, and clauses in a series. It is always proper to use the last serial comma.

   _____

   _____

3. **Interrupting words, phrases, and clauses:** Interrupting words, phrases, or clauses that make a sentence clear but do not provide essential information are usually set off by commas.

   _____

   _____

4. **To avoid misunderstanding:** Commas tell the reader which words belong together and how to read the sentence fluently. Place commas in the second sentence below to avoid confusing the reader.

   While on vacation, her family toured the capital building. She took a picture of her parents the mayor and the governor.

   Write a sentence that shows how an improperly placed comma could lead to confusion for the reader.

   _____

   _____

Punctuating Dialogue

CONVENTIONS

When writing **dialogue**, the exact words of the speaker should be enclosed in quotation marks (" ") and set off by a comma (or commas). When it is appropriate to use a question mark or an exclamation point, use that mark in place of a comma to separate the quoted material from either the speaker or information about the speaker. For example:

> Haley said, "I definitely want to go to college when I get out of high school!" when her guidance counselor asked her about her plans for the future.

Directions: Correctly punctuate each of the sentences below.

1. ___ If you bring your camera, do not forget the film ___ ___ said Margo.

2. ___ What are the chances of us arriving on time ___ ___ Carrie asked her mom.

3. ___ How exciting ___ ___ Suzanna squealed.

Begin a new paragraph when there is a new speaker in dialogue.

Rewrite the following paragraph to reflect the correct use of dialogue.

4. We should never have come here whined José. But it was your idea Billy snapped back. I don't care whose idea it was. I just want to go home pleaded José.

_____

_____

_____

_____

_____

Punctuation Power

Directions: Review the rules of **punctuation** and decide how you should punctuate each of the following sentences. Circle the letter of the best punctuation to use in place of the question mark.

1. If you want to improve your free-throw accuracy (?) you should shoot at least 100 free throws every day after practice.
    A. comma   B. semicolon   C. no punctuation

2. The first rule on this team (?) Never miss practice.
    A. comma   B. colon   C. semicolon

3. Mrs. Habben announced that she wanted to see Mr. Caruthers (?) Meg's math teacher, right after school.
    A. no punctuation   B. semicolon   C. comma

4. Zebras, giraffes, and tigers (?) these were his favorite animals.
    A. no punctuation   B. period   C. dash

5. Where do you plan on going (?) once you leave home?
    A. no punctuation   B. semicolon   C. dash

6. I would like to see the following students (?) Jorja, Helena, José, and Katie.
    A. colon   B. comma   C. period

7. All three of her children (?) Mark, Thomas, and Jon (?) went to the local university.
    A. no punctuation   B. comma   C. dash

8. Dad seldom goes to bed early (?) he is afraid he will miss out on something.
    A. no punctuation   B. semicolon   C. dash

9. When I went to the convenience store, I bought milk, bread (?) and crackers with peanut butter.
    A. semicolon   B. comma   C. period

Punctuation Power (continued)

10. Can you please hurry up (?)
    A. period   B. question mark   C. exclamation point

11. The weatherperson on TV said (?) "We might see up to an inch of rain tomorrow."
    A. period   B. comma   C. no punctuation

12. Mr. Humke said that we should all stand and sing (?) the national anthem before the concert began.
    A. quotation mark   B. dash   C. no punctuation

13. It was a dark (?) stormy night in Hamilton.
    A. comma   B. no punctuation   C. semicolon

14. Commas are used with introductory words, phrases (?) and clauses.
    A. comma   B. dash   C. no punctuation

15. There is just one thing to do at this point (?) confess to the truth.
    A. period   B. colon   C. semicolon

16. If she(?)d only admit to stealing the answer key, Ms. Dove would probably lighten her punishment.
    A. dash   B. no punctuation   C. apostrophe

17. I told the server I wanted another order of fries (?)
    A. period   B. question mark   C. exclamation point

18. Good grief (?) I forgot to bring my homework to school today.
    A. period   B. exclamation point   C. comma

19. People (?) who eat a lot of cholesterol are at risk for heart disease.
    A. comma   B. dash   C. no punctuation

20. Wow (?) What made you think you could do that and not get caught?
    A. comma   B. semicolon   C. exclamation point

Find the Misspelled Word

Directions: Circle the **misspelled word** in each sentence below. Then, write the correct spelling of the word on the line next to the sentence.

1. _____ I accidentaly knocked over a glass of water when I walked past the kitchen table.

2. _____ Mom was still three miles from home, and the car's gas guage read *empty*.

3. _____ The ad in today's Journal Star wanted someone with at least three years of experiance in the field.

4. _____ Arnie's favorite passtime is playing video games on his computer in his room.

5. _____ The heighth of the A-frame house was nearly 25 feet.

6. _____ Marci's older sister Kim became very independant when she got her own car.

7. _____ Rodney and Taylor decided to go to an Italian resturant for lunch on Saturday.

8. _____ The reccommendation of the committee was to tear down the old courthouse and build a new one on the same site.

9. _____ Students are not to leave the classroom for any reason untill they have permission from the teacher.

10. _____ Is this material relevent to the solution of the problem?

A Search for Spelling Errors

CONVENTIONS

Directions: Carefully read the story below, and circle all of the **misspelled words.** You should find 25 spelling errors.

The First Ice Cream Cone

The origine of the first ice cream cone has been controversiel for servial centuries. Some people claim that the first paper cone came from France, while others claim that metal cones were used in Germany. Then, there are people who say that the first cone's heretage belongs to an Italien genus.

Ice cream was referred to in Europse as *iced pudding*; the cones were called *wafers*. The wafers were served at the end of a meal to calm degistion. When the wafers were rolled into funnels, they could be filed with anything, including ice cream.

However, Americans like to thing that the first edibel ice cream cone was eaten right here in the United States. Italo Marchiony, who immigrated from Italy, created an edible cone for a penny a piece. He sold them from pushcarts on the streets of New York City and applied for a patient for his invention in 1903.

There is also the story of Charles Menches, who did not plan to invent the cone; it just happened. He was selling ice cream in dishes at the 1904 World's Fair in St. Louis, Missouri. On one blisterring August day, Menches's ice cream was so poplar and business so good that he ran out of dishes before noon. He had the hottest part of the day ahead of him and no way to surve his ice cream. Then, Menches had an idea.

His friend, Ernest Hamwi from Syria, was selling zalabia in a nearby booth. Zalabia is a Middle Eastern treet made from a pastrey wafer that is covered with sirup. Menches asked his friend if he could borrow some of the wafers. He rolled one and filled it with ice cream. He even put a scope on top. His criation was an instant sucess.

There is even controversey about this tale. Some say that the vendor's naim was not Charles Menches, but Abe Doumar. Whether the ice crem cone is truely American or not, millions of Americans enjoy millions of cones every year!

Pronoun-Antecedent Agreement

CONVENTIONS

Writers use pronouns to avoid repeating nouns too many times. A sentence may sound awkward if the same word is used too often.

An **antecedent** is the noun to which a pronoun refers. A **pronoun** renames or takes the place of a noun. Just as nouns and verbs must agree in number, so must pronouns and their antecedents. For example:

When *Buster* gets out of his own yard, *he* goes wild!

In the above sentence, *Buster* is the antecedent of the pronoun *he*, and both words are singular in number.

A **faulty reference** occurs when the antecedent is a different gender, person, or number than the pronoun that replaces it. For example:

The *girl* needed to have *their* own pencils.

The antecedent *girl* is singular, and *their* is plural. Below is the correct way to write the sentence.

The *girl* needed to have *her* own pencils.

Indefinite pronouns do not refer to specific persons or things. Singular indefinite pronouns must be used with singular pronouns and verbs. Examples of singular indefinite pronouns are *anybody*, *everyone*, *somebody*, *someone*, and *nobody*. Plural indefinite pronouns must be used with plural pronouns and verbs. Examples of plural indefinite pronouns are *others*, *both*, *few*, *many*, and *several*. For example:

One of the boys on the bus gave up *his* seat.
Some of the councilmembers voiced *their* opinions.

In the first sentence, the subject is singular. *One* is the antecedent, and *his* is the pronoun. The second sentence is plural. *Some* is the antecedent, and *their* is the pronoun.

Pronoun-Antedecent Agreement (continued)

In plural sentences that involve **singular pronouns**, it is appropriate to use the phrase *his or her* or just *his* or just *her* if the group is made up of all men or all women. Read the examples below.

- Incorrect: Is *everyone* pleased with *their* grade?
- Correct: Is *everyone* pleased with *his or her* grade?
    Is *everyone* pleased with *his* grade? (to a classroom of all male students)
    Is *everyone* pleased with *her* grade? (to a classroom of all female students)

The first sentence is incorrect because the indefinite pronoun *everyone* is singular, so it does not agree with the plural pronoun *their*.

Directions: Underline the antecedent in each of the sentences below. Then, circle the pronoun that agrees in number with the antecedent.

1. I become a bit afraid when our neighbors let (his, her, their) dog run loose.

2. Since it has been getting cold, I told everyone to bring (his or her, their) coat to the party.

3. The chest looks like a genuine antique, but (it, they) is really only a reproduction.

4. Lawyers often collaborate with (his, his or her, their) colleagues.

5. Typically, many students who complete all of (his or her, their) homework assignments also do well on the tests.

6. If anyone else wants to go on the field trip, (he or she, it, they) should bring a note from home tomorrow.

7. Emily and Betsy ate a very late lunch, so neither girl could finish (her, their) dinner that night.

What Should Be Capitalized?

Directions: Review the rules of **capitalization**. Circle the words that should be capitalized in the sentences below.

1. i do not plan to go anywhere on new year's eve, but i would like to go to the store and rent some movies.

2. stewart and ernie can only hope that ms. whitson does not give a pop quiz in spanish class today, because they did not study.

3. wandering aimlessly through park mall is not exactly my idea of how i want to spend my saturday afternoon.

4. my dad bought a new laptop computer yesterday, but i have not been able to use it yet.

5. the friends of the arts society will be sponsoring an art show at the local museum.

6. who said, "genius is 1% inspiration and 99% perspiration?"

7. r.h. eaks became the president and ceo of dermaflow, inc. when eldridge climer retired.

8. mardi gras in new orleans, louisiana, has long been considered america's biggest party.

9. sausage, pepperoni, mushrooms, canadian bacon, ground beef, green peppers, and mozzarella cheese are all included on the pizzas mom makes.

10. crystal lake is just north of the city limits, but we seldom go there.

11. typically, sunday through thursday is not crowded at the desert inn, but friday and saturday nights are always sold out.

Choosing the Right Verb Tense

CONVENTIONS

Verb tense shows the time that an action takes place.

- To explain what is happening right now, use the **present** tense.
    Andy *is* never late. He *watches* the clock constantly.
- To explain what has already happened, use the **past** tense.
    Andy *arrived* at the library last week before it *opened*.
- To explain what will happen, use the **future** tense.
    I doubt that Andy *will ever miss* an appointment.

Directions: Read each sentence below. Circle the letter next to the best verb tense to use in place of the question mark.

1. (?) the phone ringing? Listen!
   A. Was that   B. Is that   C. Will that be

2. When your plane (?), please give me a call.
   A. lands   B. will land   C. landed

3. Stephanie seems very (?) recently!
   A. will stress   B. stress   C. stressed

4. This party (?) not very exciting at the moment. Should we leave?
   A. will be   B. is   C. was

5. Amber's grade in math (?) bad if she doesn't turn in more of the homework assignments.
   A. was   B. is   C. will be

6. When Andy broke his leg, he (?) to stay in the hospital overnight.
   A. had   B. will have   C. is having

7. I want to go to the movies, but I (?) everything out there that I wanted to see.
   A. will have seen   B. see   C. have seen

The Correct Verb Tense

Verb tense indicates the **time** (past, present, or future) when an event takes place. It is inappropriate to shift from one tense to another if the time frame for each action is the same. For example:

> About noon the sky *darkened*, a breeze *sprang* up, and a low rumble *announces* the approaching storm.

The first two verbs, *darkened* and *sprang*, are in the past tense, but the third verb, *announces*, is in the present tense. Therefore, the sentence should be written as:

> About noon the sky *darkened*, a breeze *sprang* up, and a low rumble *announced* the approaching storm.

Directions: Rewrite each sentence below for verb-tense agreement.

1. When the sun finally sets in the western sky, the crowd grew very quiet and watch the beautiful hues in awe.

   _____

   _____

   _____

2. People will never be good editors if they did not know how to punctuate sentences well.

   _____

   _____

   _____

3. It was raining so hard that we should all run inside the shelter.

   _____

   _____

Learning to Use Similes

Directions: Read each **simile** below. On the lines provided, briefly explain what you think the simile means. Then, write a sentence that uses the simile correctly. For example:

> as blind as a bat: Since bats were once thought to be blind, whoever or whatever is being compared to a bat would not be able to see very well.—Dad's thick glasses make him look as blind as a bat.

1. as clean as a whistle: _____

_____

_____

_____

2. like coming home: _____

_____

_____

_____

3. as warm as toast: _____

_____

_____

_____

4. as big as life: _____

_____

_____

_____

Writing Metaphors

CRITICAL-THINKING SKILLS

Metaphors can be powerful tools of language. To be effective, the metaphor must not be so much of a stretch that it confuses the reader. On the other hand, drawing a comparison between things that are closely related will make the metaphor ineffective. For example:

- Effective: The kitten was a bolt of lightning streaking across the yard.
- Ineffective: The kitten was a tiger streaking across the yard.

Directions: On the lines, write an original metaphor to describe each of the topics below.

1. a quiet person: _____

_____

2. a loved one: _____

_____

3. your pet: _____

_____

4. new clothes: _____

_____

5. a favorite food: _____

_____

6. an unpleasant sound: _____

_____

7. winning a game: _____

_____

Idioms

An **idiom** is an expression that means something different than how the words in the phrase are normally used. For example, *tickled pink* means that someone is really pleased about something.

Directions: Circle each idiom in the following sentences. Then, on the lines provided write what you think the expression means.

1. His ideas put him ahead of the pack.

   _____

2. Jessica proved that she was worth her salt when she scored the winning points.

   _____

3. The scientist was back to square one after the invention failed to perform.

   _____

4. Jenny told Mary Lou that she was sure Kristi was leaving town, because she got it straight from the horse's mouth.

   _____

5. Raul was scheduled to sing the national anthem at the football game, but he got cold feet at the last minute and backed out.

   _____

6. My mom has a green thumb when it comes to house plants.

   _____

7. Michael was at loose ends until Kelly signed off of the computer.

   _____

Let's Cut a Deal

Idioms are used by writers when they want to give their readers interesting visual imagery. The caption for the picture below reads, *Richard cut a deal with his parents so that if he did the dishes, he could stay up later.* The phrase *cut a deal* does not mean that Richard did this:

Directions: You can draw your own interpretation of an idiom as well. In the space below, choose one of the idioms from the list to draw. Then, below your drawing, explain what it really means.

- bark up the wrong tree
- all thumbs
- fish out of water
- all the bells and whistles
- apple of my eye
- heart of stone
- cash cow
- bury your head in the sand

Using Proverbs

Proverbs are popular sayings, often passed down through generations, that offer advice or provide a general truth. Proverbs make the reader think. They can be an effective way to teach a lesson or to illustrate a point for the reader.

For example, the proverb *All that glitters is not gold* is a clever way of saying that everything that is attractive on the outside may not be valuable on the inside. A writer might use this proverb as inspiration for a story about a person who appeared to be a genuine friend, but was discovered to be otherwise at the end of the story.

Directions: Choose a proverb from the list below. On the lines, write a story that illustrates the meaning of the proverb you chose without including the proverb in your story. Continue on another sheet of paper if you need more room.

- Bad news travels fast.
- Do not speak of secrets in a field that is full of little hills.
- Time flies when you are having fun.
- A rose smelled too often loses its fragrance.
- A fool and his money are soon parted.
- Beauty is in the eye of the beholder.
- If it is not broken, do not fix it.
- Those who live in glass houses should not throw stones.

_____

_____

_____

_____

_____

_____

_____

Hinky-Pinkies

A **hinky-pinky** is a riddle that has two rhyming, two-syllable words as the answer. They are fun to solve, and they are just as much fun to create. The following sentence is an example of a hinky-pinky.

A written communication that has been edited is a *better letter.*

Directions: Read each of the following clues. On the line provided, write the two words that will solve the riddle.

1. a young cat in love _____

2. a person who tricks kings _____

3. a prepared stuffed bear _____

4. one who lives in a basement _____

5. an above-average knitted garment _____

6. a stationary mystery _____

7. a believable food _____

Hinkety-pinketies have two rhyming words with three syllables each as answers.

8. when a candidate loses _____

9. the White House _____

10. two drums in a conversation _____

On the lines below, come up with two hinky-pinkies of your own and try them with a friend or a parent.

_____

_____

_____

Proofreaders' Marks

Mark or Symbol	Meaning	Example
☰	Use an uppercase letter.	Mr. jones
/	Use a lowercase letter.	a Fat rabbit
℮	Delete.	ten little piggs
◡	Close the space.	the fuzz y cat
#	Insert a space.	theeagle
∼	Reverse the letters or words.	the happy dog
sp	Correct the spelling error.	refrijerator
⊙ ! ?	Add end punctuation.	The end
∧	Insert a comma.	Jim a plumber
∨	Insert an apostrophe.	The Smiths house
∨ ∨	Insert quotation marks.	Yes, I said.
¶	Start a new paragraph.	¶ The white pony

Answer Key

Pages 4–10
Answers will vary.

Page 11, From General to Specific
(newspaper) 3, 1, 5, 4, 2
(Grand Canyon) 5, 1, 4, 2, 3
(Ford Motors) 2, 1, 5, 3, 4
(The Renaissance) 2, 5, 4, 1, 3
Other answers will vary.

Pages 12–14
Answers will vary.

Page 15, Classifying Data
Order of answers may vary.
I. animals; A. vertebrates;
1. mammals; a. lions; b. cows;
2. reptiles; a. crocodiles;
b. snakes; 3. birds; a. cardinals;
b. robins; 4. amphibians; a. frogs;
b. salamanders; B. invertebrates;
1. mollusks; a. snails; b. oysters;
2. arachnids; a. spiders;
b. scorpions

Pages 16–20
Answers will vary.

Page 21, The Middle
10, 9, 3, 5, 6, 11, 13, 8, 2, 1, 4,
7, 12

Pages 22–28
Answers will vary.

Page 29, As Red as a Rose
1. I, bug under a magnifying glass (like); 2. coyote's howl, bell (as clear as); 3. Ian, bird (as free as); 4. wallet, pancake (as flat as); 5. Kelly, lark (as happy as); 6. assignment, walk in the park (like); 7. sight of land, an oasis in the desert (as welcome as); 8. Carlotta, dog (as sick as); 9. golf shot, arrow (as straight as); 10. Michelle and Carley, two peas in a pod (like)

Pages 30–35
Answers will vary.

Page 36, On the Other Hand
1. F.; 2. A.; 3. B.; 4. C.; 5. F.; 6. E.; 7. D.; 8. C.; 9. A.; 10. E.; 11. B.; 12. C.; 13. B.; 14. D.; 15. D.; 16. A.; 17. A.; 18. E.; 19. A.; 20. D.; 21. C.; 22. F.; 23. B.; 24. C. or F.

Pages 37–51
Answers will vary.

Page 52, Narrative Voice
1. 1; 2. 3; 3. 1; 4. 1; 5. 3

Pages 53–58
Answers will vary.

Answer Key

Page 59, What Part of Speech?
1. last; 2. actively; 3. won;
4. but; 5. of; 6. carefully;
7. Wow!; 8. by; 9. school;
10. anyone; 11. Homer; 12. ran;
13. to; 14. and

Page 60, The Proper Use of Commas
4. parents, mayor,
Other answers will vary.

Page 61, Punctuating Dialogue
1. "If you bring your camera, do not forget the film," said Margo.
2. "What are the chances of us arriving on time?" Carrie asked her mom. 3. "How exciting!" Suzanna squealed.
4. "We should never have come here," whined José.
"But it was your idea," Billy snapped back.
"I don't care whose idea it was. I just want to go home," pleaded José.

Pages 62–63, Punctuation Power
1. A.; 2. B.; 3. C.; 4. C.; 5. A.;
6. A.; 7. C.; 8. B.; 9. B.; 10. B.;
11. B.; 12. C.; 13. A.; 14. A.;
15. B.; 16. C.; 17. A.; 18. B.;
19. C.; 20. C.

Page 64, Find the Misspelled Word
1. accidentally; 2. gauge;
3. experience; 4. pastime;
5. height; 6. independent;
7. restaurant; 8. recommendation;
9. until; 10. relevant

Page 65, A Search for Spelling Errors
(1st paragraph) origin, controversial, several, heritage, Italian, genius; (2nd paragraph) Europe, digestion, filled; (3rd paragraph) think, edible, patent; (4th paragraph) blistering, popular, serve; (5th paragraph) treat, pastry, syrup, scoop, creation, success; (6th paragraph) controversy, name, cream, truly

Page 67, Pronoun-Antecedent Agreement
1. neighbors–their; 2. everyone–his or her; 3. chest–it; 4. lawyers–their; 5. (many) students–their;
6. anyone–he or she; 7. girl–her

Answer Key

Page 68, What Should Be Capitalized?
1. I, New Year's Eve, I; 2. Stewart, Ernie, Ms. Whitson, Spanish;
3. Wandering, Park Mall, I, Saturday; 4. My, I; 5. The Friends, Arts Society; 6. Who, Genius;
7. R.H. Eaks, CEO, Dermaflow, Inc., Eldridge Climer; 8. Mardi Gras, New Orleans, Louisiana, America's; 9. Sausage, Canadian, Mom; 10. Crystal Lake;
11. Typically, Sunday, Thursday, Desert Inn, Friday, Saturday

Page 69, Choosing the Right Verb Tense
1. B.; 2. A.; 3. C.; 4. B.; 5. C.;
6. A.; 7. C.

Pages 70–72
Answers will vary.

Page 73, Idioms
1. ahead of the pack; 2. worth her salt; 3. back to square one;
4. straight from the horse's mouth; 5. cold feet;
6. green thumb; 7. at loose ends

Pages 74–75
Answers will vary.

Page 76, Hinky-Pinkies
1. smitten kitten; 2. ruler fooler;
3. ready teddy; 4. cellar dweller;
5. better sweater; 6. paper caper;
7. credible edible;
8. election rejection;
9. President's residence;
10. percussion discussion